Virtual Danger

STAYING SAFE ONLINE

by Anne K. Brown

Content Adviser:
Billy AraJeJe Woods, Ph.D.,
Department of Psychology, Saddleback College,
Mission Viejo, California

Reading Adviser:
Alexa L. Sandmann, Ed.D.,
Professor of Literacy, College and Graduate School
of Education, Health, and Human Services,
Kent State University

Compass Point Books
151 Good Counsel Drive
P.O. Box 669
Mankato, MN 56002-0669

Photographs ©: Capstone Press/Karon Dubke, cover, 14, 31; Shutterstock/
Supri Suharjoto, 5; Michael Thompson/123RF, 6; Shutterstock/Elena Elisseeva,
7; Newscom/UPI Photo/Bill Greenblatt, 9; Dndavis/123RF, 12; AP Images/
News Sentinel, Jeff Adkins, 13; Newscom, 16; Shutterstock/Tyler Olson,
17; Shutterstock/Yuri Arcurs, 21; Orangeline/123RF, 23; AP Images/Toby
Talbot, 24; Shutterstock/Monkey Business Images, 25; Cathy Yeulet/123RF,
27, 40; AP Images/Charlie Riedel, 30; Getty Images Inc./Photo by National
Center for Missing and Exploited Children, 33; Shutterstock/goodboypictures,
34; Shutterstock/Mikhail Lavrenov, 36; Shutterstock/william casey, 38;
Shutterstock/Monika Wisniewska, 42.

Editor: Brenda Haugen
Page Production: Heidi Thompson
Photo Researcher: Marcie Spence
Art Director: LuAnn Ascheman-Adams
Creative Director: Joe Ewest
Editorial Director: Nick Healy
Managing Editor: Catherine Neitge

Library of Congress Cataloging-in-Publication Data
Brown, Anne K., 1962–
  Virtual danger : staying safe online / by Anne K. Brown.
    p. cm.—(What's the issue?)
  Includes bibliographical references and index.
  ISBN 978-0-7565-4251-1 (library binding)
  1. Internet and teenagers—Juvenile literature.
  2. Computer crimes—Juvenile literature.
  I. Title. II. Series.
  HQ799.2.I5B76 2009
  004.67'8083—dc22   2009006880

Visit Compass Point Books on the Internet at *www.compasspointbooks.com*
or e-mail your request to *custserv@compasspointbooks.com*

TABLE OF CONTENTS

CHAPTER one

YOU'RE NOT AS SAFE AS YOU THINK

Jessica* was finishing her homework on her family's computer when an e-mail message popped up from her friend Morgan. She excitedly clicked it open—and then her eyes filled with tears. The message was full of horrible insults and called her a string of nasty names. Jessica felt as if she had been hit by a bus.

She showed the e-mail message to her parents. They called Morgan's parents and discovered that Jessica's friend was visiting her grandmother, who didn't even own a computer.

Jessica was relieved to find out that Morgan hadn't sent the e-mail message, but she still felt slammed. Was it a random prank? Was someone being cruel on purpose? Not knowing made her nervous, upset, and suspicious.

* This and other names in this book have been changed for privacy reasons, except when reported in the media.

"At first I felt like someone had punched me in the stomach," Jessica said. "I've never heard language like that, and I was crushed to think my friend felt that way. I was glad to find out Morgan hadn't sent the e-mail. But the next few days at school, I kept looking at everyone suspiciously. Did anyone really feel that way about me? I was scared that someone was really out to get me."

You might wonder how something like this could happen. Well, Morgan had done something foolish—she had given her e-mail password to a few friends she thought she could trust. After this prank, she suspected that one of them had sent the nasty message—

To help ensure that no one can access your e-mail account, keep your password in a safe place and don't share it with anyone. It's also a good idea to change your password often.

or that her friends had given the password to others. Her parents helped her change her password so the prank wouldn't happen again.

The prank hit Jessica hard. Even months later, she sometimes got nervous when she checked her e-mail. "This cold shiver would come over me sometimes when I logged in," she explained. "Especially when I got e-mail from Morgan. Or if I would hear one of the nasty words in that

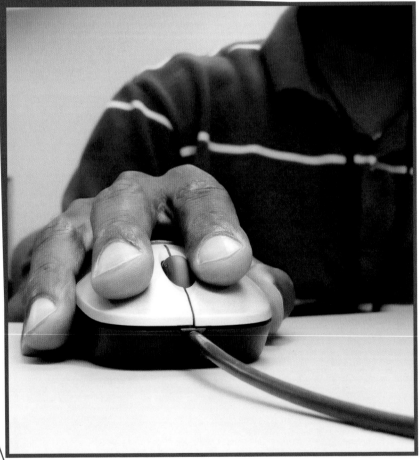

If someone is scaring you online, don't just hope the problem will go away.
Tell a trusted adult.

It's important for teens to develop friendships with people they can trust.

e-mail on TV, … I would feel like I had been slapped. It probably took eight or nine months until I had completely gotten over the whole thing."

The prank hit Morgan hard, too. She had trusted some friends with her password—and one of them had betrayed her. And she didn't know which one. She didn't know whom to trust any more.

Were Jessica and Morgan just being drama queens? Their feelings are not unusual, according to Mary Hoffmann, an assistant principal in Parker, Colorado. She says that relationships with friends are critically important for teens, and that teens are always worried about what people think of them. If teens think that their friends have turned against them, it can be devastating, Hoffmann says. Even if they are able to patch things up, they can have problems trusting other people. And those trust problems can last well into adulthood.

Wait! What Just Happened Here?

Morgan gave out her password, and someone used it to pretend to be her. Morgan got her first taste of identity theft.

Jessica was slammed by cyberbullying. Someone decided it would be fun to pick on her and upset her, and he or she did it while hiding behind a computer.

Identity theft and cyberbullying are just two of many dangers that lurk on the Internet. Lots of teens are running into trouble on the Internet. And it goes way beyond fake e-mails and mean messages.

Cruelty or Crime?

You've probably heard the story of Megan Meier, the 13-year-old girl in Dardenne Prairie, Missouri. Megan killed herself after an Internet "friend" named Josh blew her off and classmates posted nasty comments about her on MySpace. Megan's case made national headlines. Her story prompted police and lawmakers to look at Internet pranks in an entirely new way.

It turns out that Josh wasn't even real. The mother of one of Megan's schoolmates invented Josh to trick Megan. The mother's actions were calculated and cruel, but the police couldn't charge her with a crime. No laws existed that defined her behavior as criminal. After that, though, Missouri and other states began passing laws to make cyberbullying illegal.

Megan's death showed how bad cyberbullying can become. As a result of her case, cyberbullying is no longer just cruel—in many places it's criminal.

Cyberbullying is a rotten thing to do—and thanks to new laws, cyberbullies can go to prison.

Where's the Danger?

When you're at home on your computer, you probably feel

Missouri Governor Matt Blunt shook hands with Tina Meier, Megan's mom, after he signed into law a bill that protects children from Internet stalking and harassment.

pretty safe. If you're doing homework or e-mailing friends, you probably aren't thinking about criminals and others who want to harm you. But you have to be careful online, just as you would at a shopping mall or a concert. If you're on the Internet, just keep in mind that dangers such as cyberbullies, thieves, and predators may be only a few clicks away.

How do you stay safe? A teen named Abigail has one suggestion. "My mom told me that any time I want to say 'no' to someone, but I feel uncomfortable, I can blame her. A girl at my school was bugging me to add her as a friend on MySpace, but I hardly knew her. I told her that my mom has to approve anyone I add, and that she didn't know this girl. My mom isn't that strict, but the girl doesn't know that. It was easier than telling her I didn't want to add her. I've used that line lots of times online and in person."

Abigail's parents raised her to be honest and polite, but they let her know that staying safe always comes first.

> "My mom told me that any time I want to say 'no' to someone, but I feel uncomfortable, I can blame her."

Sexual Content Online

A 2006 report from the National Center for Missing and Exploited Children revealed:

- **Of youth Internet users surveyed, 4 percent were asked for nude or sexually explicit photos of themselves**
- **About 13 percent reported they were asked by a stranger to take part in sexual activity or sexual talk or to reveal personal sexual information**
- **More than one-third of youth Internet users saw sexual material that they didn't want to see**

CHAPTER two

IDENTITY THEFT

Think about this for a moment—how do your teachers and friends know who you are? It's your identity, and we each have one. Your identity includes your name, your face, your school, where you live, and other things that make you *you*.

Now imagine someone pretending to be you. Whether the person does it on paper or with a computer, it's a form of identity theft. It happens any time people pretend to be somebody they're not.

In Morgan's case, someone sent messages using her e-mail address and password. Two people were hurt by the prank—Jessica, who received the nasty e-mail messages, and Morgan, who was suspected of sending them. Luckily for Morgan, she could prove she hadn't sent them, since she was nowhere near a computer when it happened. She might have had a hard time proving her innocence if she had been home alone or at a friend's house. It could have ruined her reputation and her relationships with her friends.

Avoiding trouble isn't hard if you think ahead. Lots of families have their own rules or tips. "My parents are paranoid about staying safe," says Nicholas. "They have a rule—if I need to enter my password or home address anywhere on the Internet, they have to see the site first. It makes me feel like a little kid, but I know they're doing it to protect our family."

Public Identity

Identity damage can go way beyond mean e-mail messages and hurt feelings. People in a small town in California were upset when someone started passing around a note at a local high school about some hot pictures on a new Web site.

People who went to the Web site found pictures of teenage girls who looked as if they were drinking. They were holding plastic cups,

slumped over as if they were drunk, and lying on a bed with empty vodka bottles. Some of the girls looked as if they had passed out from drinking.

The site was called "The Boozing Babes," and the pictures had names next to them. You couldn't clearly see the faces, but

Remember that pictures you put on the Internet are there for anyone to see. Even if you remove them, you can't be sure they're gone for good.

the names belonged to girls who went to the high school.

News of the Web site spread like crazy, and soon the whole town had seen the photos. Parents freaked out, police were called, and the school held an assembly that nearly ended in a riot. Lots of reputations were damaged. One of the girls nearly lost her full scholarship to college. All of the girls who were on sports teams were suspended. Rumors and gossip about all the girls spread out of control.

The police looked into the whole nasty business, and that's when they made a startling discovery. The whole thing was a fraud. None of the girls in the photos could actually be identified. The party room turned out to be a hotel room. And the clothes worn in the pictures didn't belong to any of the girls who were named. Then suddenly, before police could make any arrests, the Web site vanished.

The town realized that it was the victim of a prank. Things settled down after a few weeks. But for about 10 days, the town was ripped apart. A lot of pain and fear and anger gripped those families.

The photos vanished, but they might not be gone forever. Once pictures have made it onto the Internet, there's no telling where or when they will turn up next.

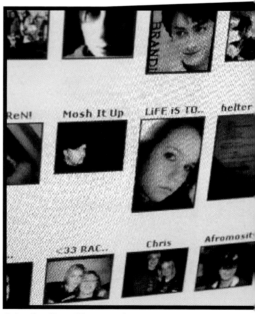

School police officers are beginning to hunt through MySpace Web pages and other social networking sites to find information on student crimes.

Photos aren't the only things that can be used against you on the Internet. Every day thieves are finding ways to rip off unsuspecting people.

Electronic Theft

Criminals have dozens of ways to get personal information, such as bank account numbers, credit card numbers, passwords, and Social Security numbers. They use this information to steal

How Is Personal Information Stolen?

The Federal Trade Commission has identified six methods that are used to steal personal information:

1. **Stealing paperwork from a trash bin**

2. **Skimming: using an electronic device to steal a credit card number when it is swiped**

3. **Phishing**

4. **Changing a victim's address to divert bills and credit card statements**

5. **Stealing credit cards and ID cards from a wallet or purse**

6. **Lying (including by phone or e-mail) in order to trick a victim out of personal information**

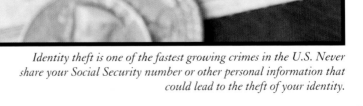

Identity theft is one of the fastest growing crimes in the U.S. Never share your Social Security number or other personal information that could lead to the theft of your identity.

money directly from checking or savings accounts. They also apply for new credit cards or take out loans—all in someone else's name. Then they go on a shopping spree, buying lots of small items or even large items such as a car or a boat. If a criminal takes out a credit card or loan in your name, *you* get stuck with the bill. You'll have to persuade the bank or credit card company to remove the charges, and that can be a real mess.

In the meantime, any phony loans or credit cards will appear on your credit score. A credit score is like a report card of your finances. Banks look at credit scores to decide whether they can trust you with a car loan or credit card. If your credit score gets messed up by thieves, it could take years to get it cleaned up. To protect yourself, be suspicious any time you get a message asking for any of this information. Ask an adult to check it out before you reply.

Don't Help the Criminals!

Sometimes victims of identity theft unknowingly help crooks steal their information. Andy fell into that trap.

While attending college near Quincy, Massachusetts, Andy maintained eBay and PayPal accounts. He received what looked like an urgent e-mail message from PayPal telling him that his account had been restricted and that he should update his information. Fol-

What Criminals Most Want

The 2006 Identity Theft Survey Report published by the Federal Trade Commission ranked the most frequent targets of identity crime as:

1. Credit cards
2. Checking and savings accounts
3. Telephone service

15

An online auction site, eBay employs about 15,500 people and is headquartered in San Jose, California.

lowing the instructions in the e-mail message, Andy filled in his checking account number and the personal identification number for his debit card.

The next day, Andy checked his bank balance and discovered that it was lower than he had expected. When he called his bank, he found that small amounts of money—$5 and $10—had been taken from his account several times, sometimes from an ATM in Spain. His bank told him he had been the victim of a phishing scheme—a phony message fishing for banking information. Andy canceled his ATM card right away, closed his checking account, and opened new accounts. To be safe, he also closed his eBay and PayPal accounts.

Andy lost about $100 from his bank account. How did he feel after all this? "I felt dumb and

Online shopping can be fun, but if you get any e-mail messages from shopping sites asking for personal information, let your parents know right away.

17

How Widespread Is Internet Crime?

In 2007 the Internet Crime Complaint Center referred more than 90,000 cases to law enforcement officials. These cases included auction fraud, credit card fraud, computer intrusions, spam, and child pornography.

tricked for even responding to the e-mail," he said. Now he's much more careful. "I would tell people not to respond to anything that asks for bank or PIN numbers so you can protect yourself. Also be suspicious of e-mails that begin 'Dear Subscriber'— anything that doesn't use your actual name. I found out that real e-mails will contain your first and last name."

> "I would tell people not to respond to anything that asks for bank or PIN numbers so you can protect yourself."

Andy was lucky—he caught the problem early. Otherwise his checking account might have been drained, or the criminals might have found other ways to use his information. His problems were fixed quickly, but in some cases, victims work for years to clear up phony accounts and restore their credit scores.

QUIZ

Which of the following schemes have been used as attempts
to steal money or identity through the Internet?

1. E-mail messages explaining that your account is on
hold until you update your personal information

2. A lottery offer asking you to pay money in order to
receive your winnings

3. A charity asking you to send money or a credit
card number

4. Offers for a free hotel stay or airfare

5. An offer to sell you an item that brings you
good luck

6. An auction selling concert tickets

7. An offer to sell an item at an unbelievably
low price

Answers:
All of these have been used as scams. Some times the concert tickets are phony. Some items may be offered at cheap
prices but come with super-high shipping costs, hidden
charges, or are damaged or worthless.

CHAPTER three

CYBERBULLYING

Cyberbullying is becoming a major problem for teens. Cyberbullying happens when a person is cruel to someone by sending or posting harmful material. It can also mean using the Internet or other technology such as cell phones to spread lies or rumors or verbally gang up on a victim.

What Counts as Bullying?

If you write or forward e-mail or text messages that are meant to be hurtful, you could be considered a cyberbully. If those messages contain words that you'd never dare let come out of your mouth or you wouldn't want your parents or teachers to hear, that could be bullying, too. If you do any of this on a regular basis, you're almost definitely a bully. Ask yourself why you do it—and stop.

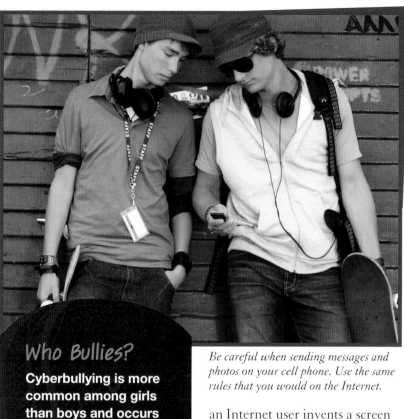

Who Bullies?

Cyberbullying is more common among girls than boys and occurs most often in the 15- to 16-year-old age group.

Be careful when sending messages and photos on your cell phone. Use the same rules that you would on the Internet.

Teens begin bullying for lots of reasons. Some think it's fun to pick on someone else. Others want to go along with the crowd or impress a popular kid. Some teens get drawn into bullying because it's anonymous. When an Internet user invents a screen name, no one knows who is behind that name. The user can say all kinds of things without anyone knowing who he or she is.

A group of 13- and 14-year-olds ran into trouble after they created a private chat room for their small class at a private school. The students had fun for a while exchanging messages. Then the fun turned to bullying, as Lauren explains: "We were such a small group that it didn't take long for us to figure out each other's screen names. Then some kids started logging in under other people's screen names. They'd make nasty comments while pretending to be somebody else. Pretty soon everyone was mad and upset. The parents shut down the chat room. Some of the kids in our class wouldn't speak to each other for weeks afterward. Nobody ever meant to bully anyone, but that's what ended up happening. Most of us couldn't believe how mean our friends could be."

What's the Big Deal, Anyway?

Bullying ended fatally for Rachael Neblett of Mount Washington, Kentucky. Rachael was a high school cheerleader and gymnast with a bubbly personality. In the summer of 2006, she

started getting threatening messages on her MySpace account.

Rachael told her sister Peyton about the messages, and Peyton told their parents. The messages weren't just ordinary curses and slams. The sender was more like a stalker. The message poster remained anonymous but could describe Rachael's daily moves, such as her activities at school.

Rachael's parents talked to the

A Bully's Tricks

Bullies know how to exploit a victim, according to Sgt. Thomas Liebenthal of the Milwaukee County Sheriff's Department in Wisconsin. He advises caution in revealing personal feelings or private information. Bullies know how to use that information to harass their targets. If bullying starts, continuing to exchange words with the bully will only prolong or raise the level of the harassment.

school principal, who assigned teachers to watch her during the day. In early October 2006, Rachael received a threatening e-mail message that said she would be put in the morgue. She was afraid to go to school or out with friends. On October 9, 2006, Rachael committed suicide. She was not being treated for depression, and she was not using drugs or alcohol. Her parents blame cyberbullying for her death. Police tracked down the computer where the e-mail messages came from but couldn't prove who wrote them. No one was ever charged with a crime.

The High Price of Being Mean

Girls aren't the only ones who suffer from cyberbullying. Another high-profile case

Don't let cyberbullies ruin your life. Wiredkids.org suggests deleting all e-mail messages—unread—from people you don't know. And don't reply to spam or harassing or offensive e-mail messages.

took place in Essex Junction, Vermont. During the summer between seventh and eighth grade, Ryan Halligan made friends online with a girl from his class. Then Ryan learned that the online friendship was just a joke. Classmates joined in and started calling him names online, and they spread rumors that he was gay. They harassed him and made fun of him.

In October of his eighth-grade year, Ryan killed himself. His parents believe their son's suicide was the direct result of bullying and cyberbullying.

Bullying was one thing when it happened in front of a few kids at school, but it was worse when instant messages were shared

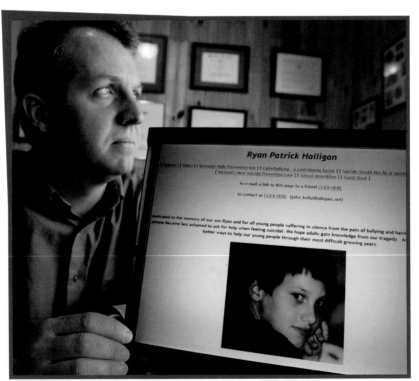

John Halligan displayed the Web site devoted to his son Ryan.

Think twice before spreading rumors or other information you see on the Internet. How would you feel if you were in that person's shoes?

Is Suicide a Real Threat?

Suicide is the third leading cause of death among people between the ages of 10 and 24. It results in about 4,500 deaths each year.

among many classmates. Ryan felt that most of his class was laughing at him.

Suicide is the most extreme outcome of cyberbullying. Thousands of kids go through depression, humiliation, and pain because of cyberbullies. They are often too afraid or embarrassed to ask for help.

Public Humiliation

Cyberbullying is especially hurtful when it's public. With e-mail and Internet cell phones, negative comments and embarrassing pictures can be sent to a lot of people in a few seconds. Teens who are bullied feel as if the whole world is against them. They wonder what is wrong with them. They might be afraid to go to school. They tend to bottle up their feelings because of embarrassment or fear.

Teen bullies don't always understand what they are doing, according to Mary Hoffmann, an assistant principal. They don't realize how much damage they can cause. For a teen who is already having problems or is depressed, a bullying incident can be the last straw.

Hoffmann says many teens forward every e-mail message they get. They do it automatically, sometimes without even reading the entire message. She has seen chain letters that threaten horrible consequences, including death, if the recipient doesn't forward them quickly to several people. Hoffmann believes that many teens are naive enough to think that the chain letter threats could be true, so they forward them. For some kids, a message like that could send them into serious depression.

Even Free Speech Has Limits

You might be thinking, "But this is the United States, and I have

The Penalties for Internet Slander

In 2002 Marianne Luban was ordered to pay $25,000 to Katherine Griffis, an Egyptology instructor at the University of Alabama. Luban spread lies about Griffis on an archaeology Internet forum and implied that Griffis' credentials were not real. Luban's lies harmed Griffis' reputation.

In 2008 Sue Scheff, a Florida lawyer, was awarded $11.3 million—the largest settlement ever in a case of Internet slander. Carey Bock had called Scheff a crook and a con artist in an online forum and damaged Scheff's reputation as a lawyer. Bock was ordered to pay for her damaging posts.

the right to free speech." Free speech, yes, but slander or libel? No. Slander is a crime in which a person says something untrue publicly that harms someone else. Libel is similar, but it deals with false comments that are written and posted publicly. When people make up lies about someone in a chat room or blog in a way that could hurt or ruin that person's reputation, they take a dangerous step toward committing slander or libel. If the victim chooses to sue, the author of those lies can be forced to pay a lot of money.

Sometimes it's hard to remember the rules when you're on the Internet with friends. Don't let others talk you into posting rumors or forwarding damaging chain letters.

More cases of Internet slander and libel will be seen in the future, according to Jill Dauska, an attorney in Los Angeles, California. She says the legal system is just beginning to understand how libel and slander operate online. Many people post comments without thinking, and they forget that their comments are public. They sometimes step over the line into slander or libel. Dauska advises teens to learn now to control themselves online. Learning good habits in the teen years will be an advantage later. When they are adults, nasty online remarks could result in being sued or getting fired from a job.

Save Someone—Right Away

If you're involved in cyberbullying, stop. If you know others who are, ask them to stop. Ask them how they would feel if it happened to them. What if their victim were to commit suicide? You might feel awkward talking about it, but it's wrong to allow someone to continue to suffer.

Pablo remembers what it was like to be bullied. "When I was in grade school, I was bullied by one kid," he said. "Most of my class didn't even know about it. Every day that kid would get in my way, just to let me know he was the boss. I could tolerate it because it was subtle. But

"But these days, when a whole class slams one kid on the Internet—I couldn't have stood up to that. It hurts to think about what a victim like that is going through."

these days, when a whole class slams one kid on the Internet—I couldn't have stood up to that. It hurts to think about what a victim like that is going through. My little brother is 15, and I tell him never to cyberbully. If he ever gets bullied, he has to come to me right away."

CHAPTER four

INTERNET PREDATORS

You've heard about Internet predators, right? Well, listen up: They're real, and they're out there. More than 2,000 kids are reported missing in the United States every day. About a quarter of those missing kids are taken by strangers. And more often than you might guess, they find their victims over the Internet.

You might hear other names for Internet predators. *Sexual predator*, *pedophile*, or *sex offender* are a few. Whatever they're called, the person behind the name has one intent, and that's to harm or have sexual contact with an unwilling person— often a kid.

What Do Predators Want?

Some predators use the Internet to look at child pornography. They even swap pornography with other predators. They might get their thrills by sending sexually suggestive messages. Some have resorted to kidnapping, sexual assault, and murder.

Sex offenders know what they want and how to get it. These criminals know to look for victims where they hang out—and for kids and teens, that means the Internet. The Internet is appealing and convenient for sex offenders because it offers privacy. A predator can access chat rooms and Web sites from home, without family members, co-workers, or neighbors ever suspecting anything.

Nancy became frightened about a friendship her 10-year-old

Are Sex Offenders Really Out There?

In the United States, more than 600,000 people are sex offenders. Of those, at least 100,000 are not registered, which is required by law. Many of them are considered missing.

"One in five girls and one in 10 boys will be sexually victimized in some way before they reach the age of 18. We know that sex offenders who target children are likely to be repeat offenders," said Ernie Allen, president and chief executive officer of the National Center for Missing and Exploited Children.

More than 1 million children are reported missing each year. Jim and Rhonda Beckford's daughter Kara disappeared from Belton, Missouri, in spring 2007.

son, Nathan, developed with a neighbor. In person the man was quiet and friendly. Nancy discovered that Nathan was instant messaging with the neighbor, sometimes for more than an hour. She thought it was strange that an adult would spend so much time online with a child.

If you ever question whether a site is appropriate, don't be afraid to check with a trusted adult.

"I sat with Nathan one night while he was instant messaging," Nancy recalls. "When the neighbor said that he had some new Hot Wheels cars and that Nathan should come over and play, I got really scared. Why would a single man buy Hot Wheels? I started making up excuses not to let Nathan online with this man. And I tried to distract him by suggesting he e-mail school friends instead. Eventually Nathan lost interest in the neighbor. I never told Nathan that I was suspicious."

Protect Our Children Act

In October 2008, the Protect Our Children Act was signed into law. It sets aside money to help law enforcement officials track down predators, makes child rescue a priority, and pays for computer software to assist in locating criminals who receive, sell, or produce child pornography.

Could You Be a Target?

Remember when you were young and your parents told you never to talk to strangers and never to accept gifts from strangers? Well, the same rules apply to the Internet. Teens sometimes forget these rules when they get online. They feel safe because they are at home. They think they can talk to anyone online because no one knows who they are or where they live. Most of the time, people you interact with on the Internet are harmless. Yet some of those strangers have one goal in mind: to gain the trust of a child or teen and then find a way to use them or hurt them.

Predators often find victims by joining chat rooms. Sometimes a predator will invent a screen name and pretend to be a teen to fit in with the chat room. As the predator gets to know the kids in the room, one teen might stand out as a potential target. How does the predator choose him or her? Predators are always looking for an opening, explains Roger E. Moore, a mental health counselor at a psychiatric hospital in Kentucky. If predators detect any sort of vulnerability, they go after it.

These criminals look for kids who are bored, lonely, shy, depressed, withdrawn, or having problems at home or school. They might target a teen who says he or she spends lots of time alone. Once the predator chooses a target, he works to gain the victim's trust.

Are Strangers Really Dangerous?

A February 2008 article from Reuters news service reported that the vast majority of sex offenders approached their victims with the clear intention of looking for sex. Teens who had strangers on their buddy lists, responded to strangers, or were willing to talk about sex with strangers were likely to be targeted by predators.

A Predator's Tricks

Sexual predators know how to connect with a victim. They can easily talk or write to sound like a teen; this helps put the victim at ease. Predators act concerned about their targets and pretend that they care. They are good listeners, always seem interested, and are eager to chat with their potential victims.

If a predator is interested in you, he or she will know how to use flattery to make you feel good. He or she might try to give you money or buy you gifts such as

Nonfamily Abduction

LINDSEY RYAN

TERRY DRAKE

DOB: dec-12-1988
Missing: mar-01-2003
Age Now: 14 years
Sex: F Height: 5'0" - 152 cm
Weight: 105 lbs - 48 kg
Hair: Blonde
Eyes: Blue
Missing From:
JONES
MI
USA

Abductor
DOB: feb-21-1947
Sex: M
Hair: Grey
Eyes: Hazel
Height: 6'2" - 188 cm
Weight: 190 lbs - 86 kg

The middle photo shows what Lindsey would look like if her hair was dyed black. She was last seen at her home on March 1, 2003. She is believed to be in the company of Terry Drake. A felony warrant was issued for Terry Drake on March 2, 2003. They may be traveling in a 1995 white Dodge Dakota pickup truck with Indiana license plates 406211A or 229929A. The abductor may or may not wear glasses and he has multiple tattoos on his neck and forearms. He may also use the alias name Alfonzo Devette and may use an alias DOB of 2/22/1947. CAUTION ADVISED: The abductor may be armed and dangerous.

Web sites like this one for the National Center for Missing and Exploited Children are filled with information about kids and teens who have been abducted. Lindsey Ryan was found, and her abductor was sentenced to 25 years in federal prison.

CDs or electronics. A predator might offer to fix any problems you have with parents or at school.

The predator might eventually offer pornography to you to help you feel that sexual contact is safe, acceptable, or exciting. It's not! At some point, the predator will try to be alone with you in order to follow through on his or her sexual urges. Don't fall for it, even if the person claims to be in love with you.

"I met a guy in a chat room

Never agree to get together with someone you've met online. People can appear to be anyone and any age online, but that doesn't mean they're being honest with you.

who said he was 15, like me," says Erin. "At first it was cool. But then he started asking what I looked like. One night he said, 'I'll bet you're gorgeous.' Then he asked for my bra size. I was so freaked out! He kept asking me questions, and I didn't know what to do. Finally I typed: 'This is Erin's mother. Leave her alone or I will call the police.' I never heard from that creep again."

An Internet predator will try to convince you that he or she is safe to talk to. Ultimately the predator will try to meet you. Predators have been known to send bus or plane tickets to their victims and to encourage them to run away from home so they can meet each other. Sometimes a victim thinks he or she is going to meet an online friend but ends up in the hands of a sex offender. Other times victims go with the intention of

> "I was so freaked out! He kept asking me questions, and I didn't know what to do."

participating in sexual activity. Either way these are dangerous situations, and these runaways sometimes end up dead.

Outright Threats

Some predators want the power that comes with scaring or threatening others. Aaron received a late-night instant message that said, "How are you?" Aaron IMed back and asked who the sender was. After a few questions, the sender said he must have used the wrong address—but he kept asking Aaron questions. Aaron said, "Around the sixth message, the guy asked me where I was. That was really creepy, so I said I had to go. Then the guy sent another message that he was going to find me and kill me and my family. He said he was getting on a plane to come after me." Aaron

If you get a message online that makes you uncomfortable, don't erase it. Show it to a trusted adult.

went to his mother right away, and she called the police.

The police sent a message back and told the sender to stop immediately. Aaron was told that if he got more messages, the police would look for the sender. The sender IMed back that it was all a joke, and Aaron never heard from the person again.

Aaron was lucky, but the incident was still scary. He was glad he hadn't revealed where he lived. His advice for anyone who gets a weird message? "Listen to your feelings. If something feels wrong, make them stop—or log off yourself. Ask for help from an adult right away."

CHAPTER five

HOW TO STAY SAFE

The golden rule of Internet safety is this: Trust your gut. If anything ever feels wrong to you, tell a trusted adult as soon as possible. If you ever get a message or comments in a chat room that worry or scare you, ask an adult to look at it. Log off if you need to. Your safety is more important than being rude by not answering someone.

Remember that you don't have to answer online messages immediately. Often when people read a message, they feel that they must answer right away. But the sender doesn't know when you've read the message. If a message makes you uncomfortable, close it. Then you can think about it or ask for help.

Predators may ask for your school's name or where your parents work. Don't give out this information, because they can use it to find you.

Social Networking Sites

Web sites such as MySpace and Facebook have become popular in recent years. If you join a social networking site, understand why you are doing it. If you use it to connect with friends, that's great. If you start talking with or writing to strangers, trouble could follow.

Remember that your page is not a scorecard. Don't connect

Steer Clear of Strangers

Sgt. Thomas Liebenthal of the Milwaukee County Sheriff's Department offers his top three online safety tips:

1. Never give out personal identifying information that would allow someone to find you.

2. Never arrange to meet someone in person. This is the most dangerous thing a teen could ever do. You never truly know with whom you are dealing.

3. Remember that people may not be who they seem to be. Online a predator can be any age, sex, race, religion, or ethnicity. A predator can create a phony character easily and can post fake pictures or fake a "live" webcam. Online you never really know to whom you are speaking or writing.

with people just so you can have hundreds of friends linked to you. You wouldn't pick names at random from the phone book and call them, right? Picking people from their Web photos is pretty much the same thing. If you don't know them, they aren't really friends, are they? Jonathan made that discovery. He accepted every invitation on his Facebook page and made dozens of invitations himself—mostly to girls—until he had more than 400 contacts. "I thought I was really cool because I had more contacts than any of my friends," he said. "Sometimes, if I found someone else with lots of contacts, I'd go and invite more people just to stay ahead. Then a friend asked why I did this. All of a sudden, the bubble burst and I realized it was a useless collection of names. I stopped, and even deleted some people from my list."

"I thought I was really cool because I had more contacts than any of my friends."

Treat Your Profile With Care

Let's say you join Facebook or a similar site. You'll be able to post a photo of yourself and custom-ize your page. Some people post photos of themselves smoking, drinking, acting crazy, or mak-ing rude gestures. But remember that some of this information is public. A good rule of thumb is to remember the four P's: Never post anything that you wouldn't want your parents, principal, a predator, and the police to see.

Now jump ahead into the future five years or more. Your future college, future employer, future spouse, and even future children could see what you posted about yourself. Think about what might be embarrassing later, even if it seems funny now.

Veronica discovered the dangers of her MySpace page. When she was 16, she posted that she was 18 and put up photos of herself that looked as if she were drinking—she was laughing and holding a plastic cup. She got invitations from guys in their 20s with offers like, "You look like a party girl—let's hook up." That was a huge reality check. "I was 16, and I'd never even tasted beer. All these guys were suddenly inviting me to party, and they were hinting that they wanted more. It really scared me, and I deleted my entire page."

Stay in the Real World

Teens think it's cool to go online or communicate electronically. Ask yourself—are IMs and chat rooms better than the real world? Instead of sitting at the computer, consider going to the mall, playing games, or having a sleepover. Think about times when you've had a blast with friends—you were probably together somewhere, not sending messages back and forth.

Stay Away From Adult Material

Stick with Web sites that are appropriate for your age. You might feel grown up and ready for material for older teens or adults, but it just isn't safe. You wouldn't try to go to a bar or nightclub. Those places are for adults, and not all the adults in those places are safe for kids. The same is true of adult sites and chat rooms.

Calling friends and hanging out is more fun than sitting at home alone and sending messages on your computer.

Protect Your Information

With predators, bullies, and thieves in cyberspace, you need to protect your personal information. Here's a list of things that you should *never* share online:

- Your last name
- Your address and phone number (including cell phone number)
- The name of your school, church, workplace, or places you hang out—a predator might be able to track you by finding those places
- Your Social Security number, bank account numbers, or any information about your money
- Your online passwords
- Photos that could give clues about where you live (landmarks or names of streets or buildings)
- An adult's credit card information (Never use a credit card online without asking the owner's permission.)

Protecting Your Privacy

The Children's Online Privacy Protection Act was passed in 2000. COPPA was designed to regulate the types of information that Web sites can collect about users. COPPA states that Web sites may not collect last names, addresses, phone numbers, e-mail addresses, and other information from children that might allow a person to identify and locate them. If you ever visit a Web site that asks for this information, check with an adult before continuing.

If You Get Into Trouble

Even if you try to be safe, predators or criminals could find you, just as they found Andy, Aaron, Veronica, and Erin. If this happens, stay calm. Tell a trusted adult. If you get a nasty e-mail message, text message, or IM, do not delete it. It might help track the person down.

Depending on the danger, you or an adult might need to call the police. Try to remember everything as clearly as you

Follow the Four R's

The Web site i-SAFE suggests a four-step plan for dealing with Internet problems:

RECOGNIZE techniques used by online predators to deceive.

REFUSE requests for personal information.

RESPOND assertively if you are ever in an uncomfortable situation online. Exit the program, log off or turn off the computer, tell a trusted adult, or call the police.

REPORT to a trusted adult any suspicious or dangerous contact that makes you feel uncomfortable.

Surfing the Internet can be fun and even educational if you follow the rules to stay safe.

can. Explain the situation to the police step by step.

Even if you made a mistake and gave out information or visited a site that is off limits, ask for help. It's better to admit that you messed up than to receive threats, lose money, or have a predator stalking you.

Surf Safely

The Internet is loaded with good information, great Web sites, fun games, and excellent educational material. By taking a few precautions, you'll be able to learn and have fun online. With any luck, you'll never encounter these problems. If you do, remember the tips outlined in this book. They could save your self-esteem, your bank account, or your life.

QUIZ

Ask yourself what you would do in these situations:

1. You get an e-mail message or IM from a stranger asking where you live.

2. You get an e-mail message claiming that you won a lottery. To collect your winnings, you must give a credit card number so they can send the money to your account.

3. An e-mail message arrives promising scholarship information if you'll fill in a little information.

4. Someone you know sends an e-mail message full of horrible insults and curse words.

5. You click on a Web site link and pornographic pictures pop up on your screen.

6. You discover a chat room where kids are slamming one of your classmates.

The correct behavior in all these situations: Don't respond. Tell a trusted adult as soon as possible. All of these situations pose possible dangers, and an adult can help you avoid them safely.

GLOSSARY

chain letter | e-mail message or letter that tells the recipient to copy the letter and forward it to a specified number of people; these letters often promise a reward for forwarding the message or a punishment or bad luck for failing to pass it along

fraud | action intended to trick a person into giving up money or valuables

IM (instant message) | text message exchanged in real time

libel | crime in which a person publicly writes something untruthful about another person with the intent of damaging the victim's reputation

phishing | sending fake e-mail messages that appear to have been sent by a reliable company and asking for personal information, such as bank account numbers

pornography | pictures or movies showing sexual behavior

predator | person who seeks to have sexual contact with an unwilling person or to harm that person in some other way

slander | crime in which a person publicly makes false oral statements about another person in order to damage the victim's reputation

WHERE TO GET HELP

Boys Town National Hotline
14100 Crawford St.
Boys Town, NE 68010
800/448-3000
*Trained counselors are available anytime
to assist with problems of any nature. The
hotline is open to girls and boys.*

Identity Theft Resource Center
P.O. Box 26833
San Diego, CA 92196
858/693-7935
*This nonprofit organization is dedicated
to identifying and helping people understand identity theft. It offers educational
resources and provides victim assistance.*

i-SAFE Inc.
5900 Pasteur Court, Suite 100
Carlsbad, CA 92008
760/603-7911
*A nonprofit foundation dedicated to
protecting youth while online, i-SAFE
provides resources and training for
teachers, parents, students, and law
enforcement officials.*

**National Center for Missing
and Exploited Children**
Charles B. Wang International
Children's Building
699 Prince St.
Alexandria, VA 22314-3175
800/843-5678
*The center provides resources to educate
parents and children about sexual exploi-
tation and general safety, maintains a
database of missing children, and supports
efforts to locate missing children.*

National Center for Victims of Crime
2000 M St. N.W., Suite 480
Washington, DC 20036
202/467-8700
800/394-2255
*The center's Teen Victim Project offers
free fact sheets for handling many Internet
dangers, as well as resources for reporting
all types of crime.*

SOURCE NOTES

Chapter 1
Page 5, column 1, line 1: Jessica. Portland, Oregon. Telephone interview. 22 Sept. 2008.
Page 6, column 2, line 2: Ibid.
Page 10, column 1, line 15: Abigail. Fargo, North Dakota. Personal interview. 30 Nov. 2008.

Chapter 2
Page 12, column 1, line 3: Nicholas. Rockford, Illinois. Telephone interview. 29 Nov. 2008.
Page 17, column 2, line 4: Andy. Quincy, Massachusetts. Personal interview. 12 Oct. 2008.

Chapter 3
Page 22, column 1, line 2: Lauren. Madison, Wisconsin. Telephone interview. 8 Oct. 2008.
Page 28, column 2, line 8: Pablo. Austin, Texas. E-mail interview. 25 Nov. 2008.

Chapter 4
Page 31, line 13: Nancy. Green Bay, Wisconsin. E-mail interview. 16 Nov. 2008.
Page 34, column 2, line 7: Erin. Kalamazoo, Michigan. E-mail interview. 11 Nov. 2008.
Page 35, column 2, line 10: Aaron. Albuquerque, New Mexico. Telephone interview. 21 Oct. 2008.
Page 36, column 2, line 5: Ibid.

Chapter 5
Page 39, column 1, line 10: Jonathan. Seattle, Washington. E-mail interview. 20 Nov. 2008.
Page 40, column 1, line 2: Veronica. St. Paul, Minnesota. E-mail interview. 18 Nov. 2008.

Fiction

Haddix, Margaret Peterson. *Double Identity*. New York: Simon & Schuster Books for Young Readers, 2005.

Harrison, Lisi. *The Clique*. New York: Little, Brown, 2004.

Hopkins, Cathy. *Teen Queens & Has-Beens*. New York: Simon Pulse, 2004.

McNeal, Laura, and Tom McNeal. *Crushed*. New York: Knopf, 2006.

Pixley, Marcella. *Freak*. New York: Farrar, Straus and Giroux, 2007.

Vande Velde, Vivian. *Remembering Raquel*. Orlando, Fla.: Harcourt, 2007.

Ziegler, Jennifer. *How Not to Be Popular*. New York: Delacorte Press, 2008.

Nonfiction

Breguet, Teri. *Frequently Asked Questions About Cyberbullying*. New York: Rosen Publishing, 2007.

Goodstein, Anastasia. *Totally Wired: What Teens and Tweens Are Really Doing Online*. New York: St. Martin's Griffin, 2007.

Newman, Matthew. *You Have Mail: True Stories of Cybercrime*. New York: Franklin Watts, 2008.

Internet Sites

FactHound offers a safe, fun way to find Internet sites related to this book. All of the sites on FactHound have been researched by our staff.

Here's all you do:
    Visit *www.facthound.com*
FactHound will fetch the best sites for you!

INDEX

ABOUT THE AUTHOR

Anne K. Brown holds a bachelor's degree in communication from the University of Wisconsin–Milwaukee. She has been editing and writing professionally for more than 20 years. For eight of those years, she served as an editor for the largest producer of fantasy role-playing games in the United States and was continually involved in research regarding the habits of children from 11 to 17 years old. This is her sixth book. Brown lives with her husband and daughters in West Allis, Wisconsin. As the mother of two daughters, she has a personal interest in matters of child safety. Brown serves on a number of committees and is actively involved in her local Girl Scout council.

ABOUT THE CONTENT ADVISER

Billy AraJeJe Woods has a doctorate in psychology, a master's degree in education, and a bachelor's degree in psychology. He has been counseling individuals and families for more than 25 years. He is a certified transactional analysis counselor and a drug and alcohol abuse counselor. A professor of psychology at Saddleback College, Mission Viejo, California, Woods teaches potential counselors to work with dysfunctional families and special populations. He began his counseling career in the military, where he worked with men and women suffering from post-traumatic stress disorder. In his practice, Woods has worked with many young adults.